THE GUITAR MAN ACADEMY
CONTENTS

THE GUITAR MAN ACADEMY INDUCTION!

"HEY KIDS, I'M GUITAR MAN! WELCOME TO THE GUITAR MAN ACADEMY! HERE AT THE GUITAR MAN ACADEMY YOU'LL START YOUR TRAINING TO BECOME A SUPERHERO ON THE GUITAR!

YOU'LL LEARN HOW TO SUMMON THE POWER OF THE POWER CHORD FROM THE TIPS OF YOUR FINGERS!

SO WHAT ARE YOU WAITING FOR?

IT'S TIME TO START YOUR GUITAR SUPERHERO TRAINING, SO LET'S GO!"

WRITE YOUR INITIALS HERE

PARTS OF THE GUITAR

USE THE KEY ON THE LEFT HAND SIDE TO HELP IDENTIFY WHAT EACH PART OF THE GUITAR IS CALLED. MATCH THESE NUMBERS WITH THE NUMBERS ATTACHED TO THE GUITAR ON THE RIGHT HAND SIDE.

KEY

1: HEADSTOCK
2: TUNING PEGS
3: NUT
4. FRET BOARD
5 FRET WIRE
6 NECK (BEHIND)
7: STRINGS
8 PICKUP
9: TREMOLO ARM
10: PICKUP SELECTOR
11: VOLUME CONTROL
12: TONE CONTROL
13: BRIDGE
14: GUITAR CABLE INPUT

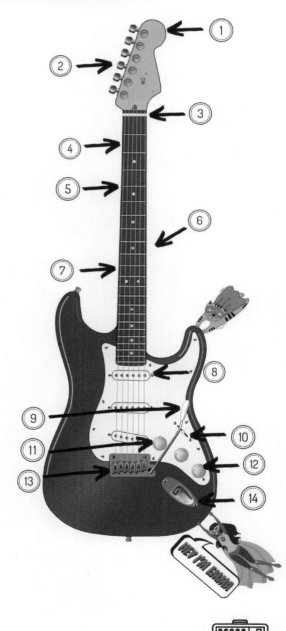

2

HOW TO HOLD A GUITAR

THERE ARE MANY WAYS TO HOLD YOUR GUITAR. THE WAY I WOULD SUGGEST IS TO TRY AND STAND UP WHEN YOU'RE PLAYING. YOU WILL NEED A GUITAR STRAP TO DO THIS. WHEN STANDING TRY TO MAKE SURE THE GUITAR IS AROUND THE AREA OF YOUR BELLY BUTTON, JUST LIKE HARRY IS HOLDING HIS GUITAR BELOW.

THEN, SIMPLY REST YOUR FOREARM ON THE CURVE OF THE BODY JUST ABOVE THE STRINGS. NEXT, SUPPORT THE NECK BY RESTING IT IN YOUR LEFT HAND (IF YOU'RE LEFT HANDED SIMPLY REVERSE THIS).

HEY I'M HARRY

3

THE STRINGS

UP NEXT YOU'LL NEED TO LEARN THE NAMES OF EACH STRING.

TRY TO FIND EACH OF THE STRINGS BELOW ON YOUR GUITAR.

STRING 6
OR THE THICK E STRING

STRING 5
OR THE A STRING

STRING 4
OR THE D STRING

STRING 3
OR THE G STRING

STRING 2
OR THE B STRING

STRING 1
OR THE THIN E STRING

HEY I'M MYA

4

HOW TO HOLD A PIC

PICS COME IN MANY DIFFERENT SIZES, SO IT MAY BE WORTH PURCHASING A SELECTION OF SIZES TO TRY OUT, BUT IN GENERAL SOMETHING AROUND 0.78MM THICK WOULD BE SUITABLE.

PLACE THE THUMB OF YOUR RIGHT HAND ON THE MIDDLE OF ONE SIDE OF THE PIC AND THEN PLACE YOUR INDEX FINGER ON THE MIDDLE OF THE OTHER SIDE WITH THE POINTY PART FACING AWAY FROM YOUR PALM.

IF YOU'RE LEFT HANDED REVERSE THIS!

GUITAR MAN!

HEY I'M ISABELLA

I'M MIA

5

HOW TO STRUM THE GUITAR

TO STRUM THE STRINGS CORRECTLY, SIT THE TIP OF YOUR PIC ON THE THICKEST STRING WITH YOUR THUMB ON THE SIDE FACING YOUR FACE.

THEN, GLIDE (STRUM) THE PIC DOWN ALL THE STRINGS FROM THE THICK STRING TO THE THIN STRING LIGHTLY, MAKING SURE ALL MOTION COMES FROM YOUR WRIST.

MAKE SURE YOU DON'T HOLD THE PIC TOO TIGHT!

WHEN YOU STRUM YOUR STRINGS, YOUR PALM SHOULD BE FACING THE STRINGS, LIKE THE PICTURE BELOW.

I'M NOAH

I'M EMILY

6

WHEN YOU PUSH DOWN ON THE GUITAR STRINGS, MAKE SURE YOU ARE PUSHING DOWN WITH THE CENTRE OF THE TIPS OF YOUR FINGERS ONLY.

THE CORRECT PLACE TO PUSH YOUR FINGERS

IT'S IMPORTANT TO PUSH DOWN ON THE CORRECT PART OF THE FRET SPACE.

THE CHORD DIAGRAM BELOW IS TELLING YOU TO PUSH FRET SPACE 2 DOWN ON STRING 5. WHEN YOU DO THIS, YOU MUST MAKE SURE YOU PUSH DOWN IN THE MIDDLE OF FRET SPACE 2 OF STRING 5 (THE SECOND THICKEST STRING). TRY THIS WITH TIP OF YOUR INDEX FINGER. NEVER PUSH ON THE FRET WIRE!

CHORD DIOGRAM

UNDERSTANDING A CHORD CHART
THE VERTICAL LINES

THE VERTICAL LINES REPRESENT THE STRINGS ON THE GUITAR AS SEEN BELOW. THE 6 REPRESENTS STRING 6, THE 5 REPRESENTS STRING 5 AND SO ON.

UNDERSTANDING A CHORD CHART
THE PARALLEL LINES

THE PARALLEL LINES REPRESENT THE FRET WIRES ON THE GUITAR. THE THICK BLACK LINE AT THE TOP REPRESENTS THE NUT.

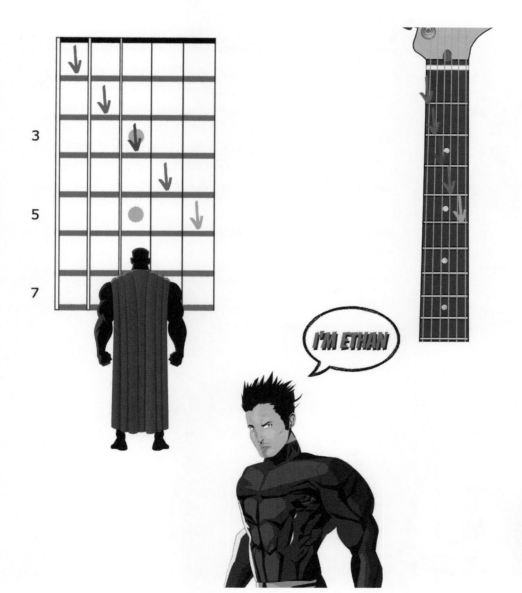

UNDERSTANDING A CHORD CHART
THE O'S AND X'S

ON THE CHORD CHART THE X'S MEAN DON'T PLAY THESE STRINGS AND THE O'S MEAN PLAY THESES STRINGS OPEN.

THIS CHORD CHART IS TELLING YOU TO STRUM STRINGS 1, 2 AND 3 (THE THINNEST STRINGS), BUT NOT 4, 5 AND 6 (THE THICKEST STRINGS). GIVE THIS A GO.

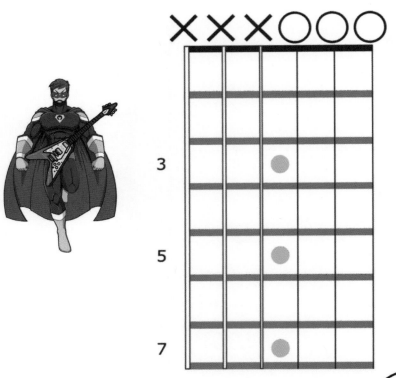

HI I'M HARVEY

UNDERSTANDING A CHORD CHART
THE CIRCLE'S

THE CIRCLE THAT THE RED ARROW IS POINTING TO IS
TELLING YOU WHERE TO PUT YOUR FINGER(S).
IN THIS CASE YOU WILL NEED TO PLACE THE TIP OF
YOUR INDEX FINGER ONTO FRET SPACE 2 OF STRING 5.

UNDERSTANDING A CHORD CHART
THE NUMBERS IN THE CIRCLES

THE NUMBERS ARE SUGGESTING WHAT FINGER(S) TO USE WHEN IT COMES TO PUSHING DOWN ON THE STRINGS.

ON THE CHORD CHART ON THE RIGHT HAND SIDE, IT'S TELLING YOU TO PUSH FRET SPACE 2 ON STRING 5 USING THE TIP OF FINGER 1.

FINGER POSITIONS

UNDERSTANDING A CHORD CHART
THE 3, 5 AND 7

THE NUMBERS ON THE-LEFT HAND SIDE OF THE CHORD CHART ARE FRET MARKER INDICATORS.

FOR EXAMPLE THE 3 IS NEXT TO FRET 3, THE 5 IS NEXT TO FRET 5 AND THE 7 IS NEXT TO FRET 7. THIS CAN BE REALLY HELPFUL WHEN FIGURING OUT WHAT FRET(S) TO PUSH DOWN.

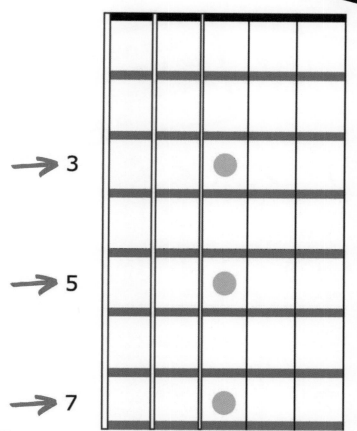

14

OPEN E5
POWER CHORD

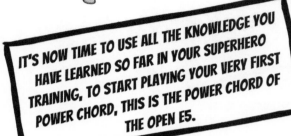

IT'S NOW TIME TO USE ALL THE KNOWLEDGE YOU HAVE LEARNED SO FAR IN YOUR SUPERHERO TRAINING, TO START PLAYING YOUR VERY FIRST POWER CHORD, THIS IS THE POWER CHORD OF THE OPEN E5.

TO PLAY THE OPEN E5 POWER CHORD PLACE THE TIP OF FINGER 1 ONTO FRET 2 OF STRING 5 AND THEN STRUM STRINGS 6 AND 5 TOGETHER.

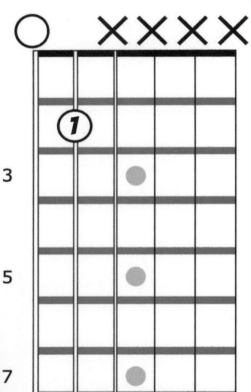

15

OPEN A5 POWER CHORD

IT'S NOW TIME TO LEARN YOUR NEXT POWER CHORD. THIS IS KNOWN AS THE POWER CHORD OF THE OPEN A5.

TO PLAY THE OPEN A5 POWER CHORD PLACE THE TIP OF FINGER 1 ONTO FRET 2 OF STRING 4 AND THEN STRUM STRINGS 5 AND 4 TOGETHER.

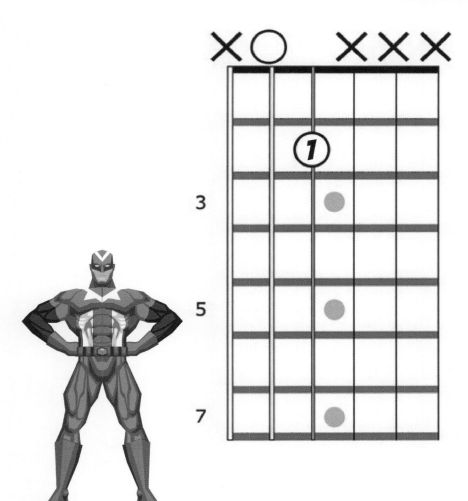

OPEN D5
POWER CHORD

NOW TIME TO LEARN YOUR FINAL OPEN POWER CHORD. THIS IS THE OPEN D5 POWER CHORD.

TO PLAY THE OPEN D5 POWER CHORD PLACE THE TIP OF FINGER 1 ONTO FRET 2 OF STRING 3 AND THEN STRUM STRINGS 3 AND 4 TOGETHER.

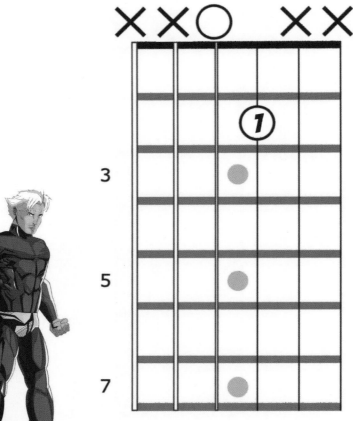

17

CHANGING BETWEEN THE OPEN E5, A5 AND D5

HAVE A GO AT PLAYING THE OPEN E5 ONCE, THEN PLAY THE OPEN A5 ONCE AND THEN PLAY THE OPEN D5 ONCE.

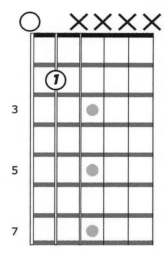

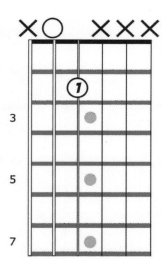

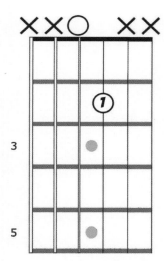

A5
POWER CHORD

TO PLAY THE A5
1) PLACE THE TIP OF FINGER 1 ONTO FRET 5 OF STRING 6

2) PLACE THE TIP OF FINGER 3 ONTO FRET 7 OF STRING 5 THEN STRUM STRINGS 6 AND 5 TOGETHER.

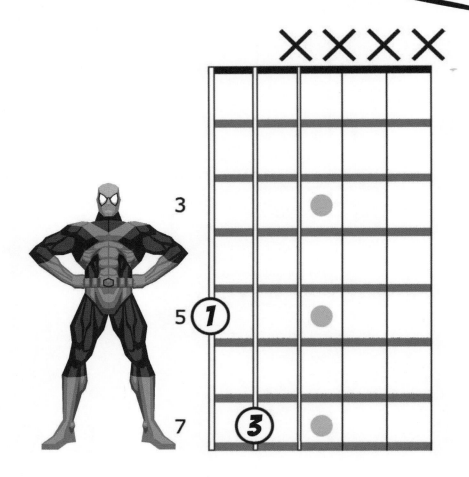

19

D5 POWER CHORD

IT'S NOW TIME TO LEARN THE D5 POWER CHORD!
1) PLACE THE TIP OF FINGER 1 ONTO FRET 5 OF STRING 5

2) PLACE THE TIP OF FINGER 3 ONTO FRET 7 OF STRING 4 AND STRUM STRINGS 5 AND 4 TOGETHER.

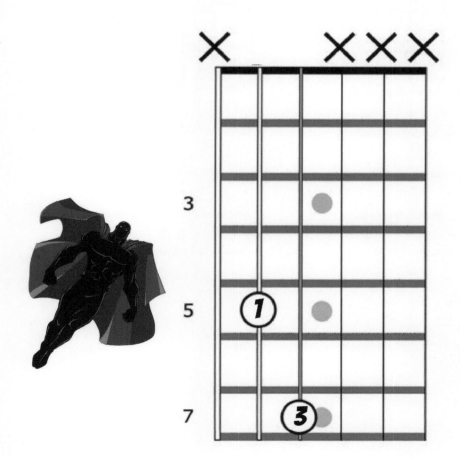

CHANGING BETWEEN THE A5 AND D5 POWER CHORD

HAVE A GO AT PLAYING BETWEEN THE A5 AND D5 POWER CHORDS.

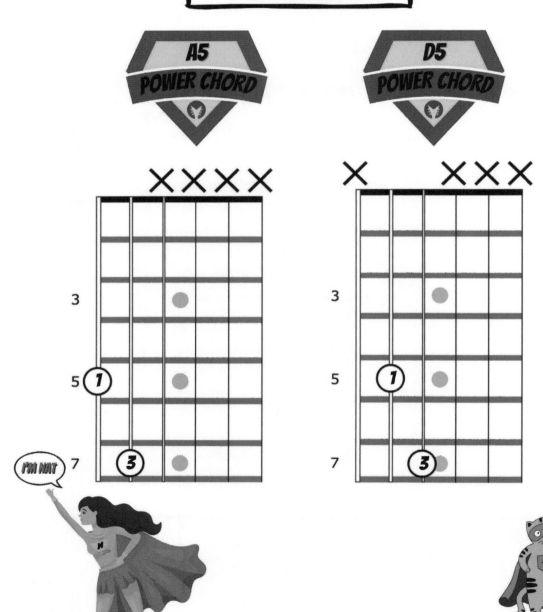

THE F5 AND A#5 POWER CHORD

THE F#5 AND B5 POWER CHORD

HAVE A GO AT LEARNING AND THEN PLAYING BETWEEN THE F#5 AND THE B5 POWER CHORDS.

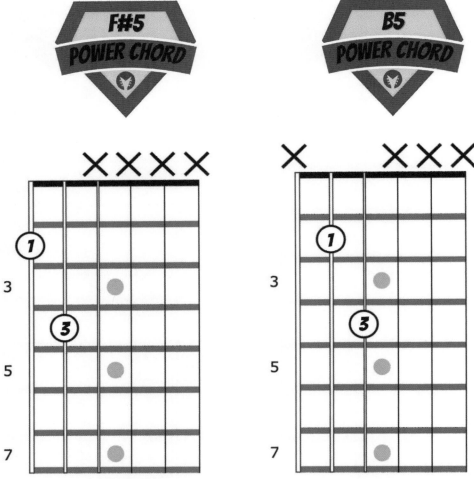

THE G5 AND C5 POWER CHORD

HAVE A GO AT LEARNING AND THEN PLAYING BETWEEN THE G5 AND THE C5 POWER CHORDS.

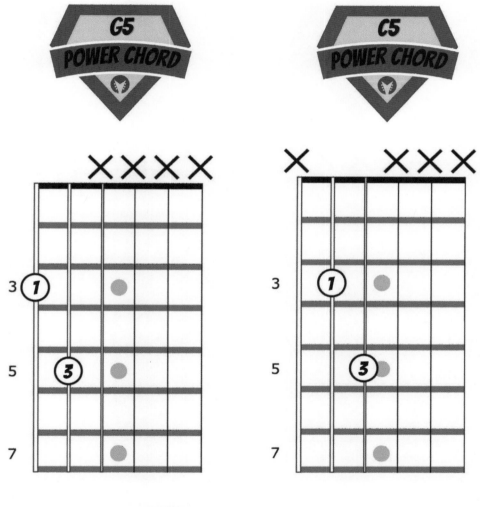

THE G#5 AND C#5 POWER CHORD

HAVE A GO AT LEARNING AND THEN PLAYING BETWEEN THE G#5 AND THE C#5 POWER CHORDS.

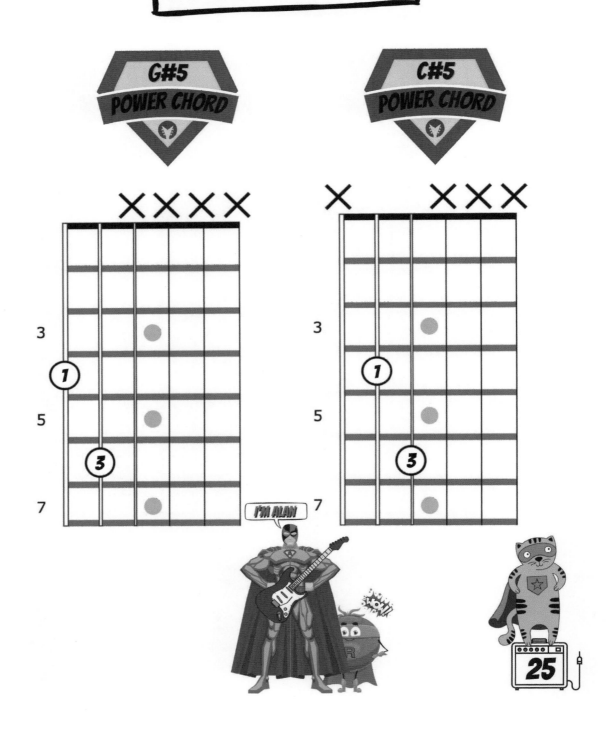

THE A#5 AND D#5 POWER CHORD

HAVE A GO AT LEARNING AND THEN PLAYING BETWEEN THE A#5 (THIS IS ANOTHER VARIATION OF THE A#5) AND THE D#5 POWER CHORDS.

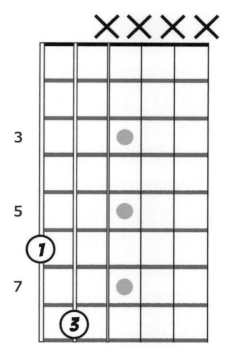

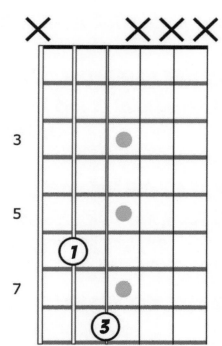

TRAINING COMPLETE!

CONGRATULATIONS! YOU HAVE NOW COMPLETED YOUR TRAINING TO BECOME A GUITAR POWER CHORD SUPERHERO AND ARE ONE STEP CLOSER TO BECOMING A GUITAR SUPERHERO JUST LIKE GUITAR MAN!

IT'S NOW TIME TO USE YOUR TRAINING AND START USING THE POWER CHORDS YOU HAVE LEARNT IN THIS TRAINING COURSE TO PLAY ALONG TO YOUR FAVOURITE SONGS.

KEEP AN EYE OUT FOR MORE GUITAR MAN ACADEMY TRAINING COURSES COMING SOON, AND DON'T FORGET TO CHECK OUT THE GUITAR MAN ACADEMY AT WWW.BANDSKILLS.COM FOR EXTRA CONTENT!

ON THE NEXT PAGE YOU WILL RECEIVE YOUR OFFICIAL GUITAR MAN ACADEMY CERTIFICATE IN POWER CHORDS.

27

THIS IS TO CERTIFY THAT

....

HAS COMPLETED THEIR
GUITAR SUPERHERO TRAINING IN
POWER CHORDS

AT
THE GUITAR MAN ACADEMY

ON

....

Printed in Great Britain
by Amazon

16716148R00018